For Noah and Talia

Now That We're Here

Elizabeth Rees

Dear Austin,
Thank you so much
for all your support of
my work and for
contributing a smart
and generous blurb
to this little book—
I so appreciate it!
Warmly,
Liz Rees
May 2009

Now That We're Here

ISBN 13: 978-1-934828-01-4

Spire Press, 532 LaGuardia Pl, Ste 298, New York, NY 10012
www.spirepress.org

ACKNOWLEDGMENTS

Poems in this manuscript originally appeared or will appear in the following journals:

CIMARRON REVIEW "Morning Drive to Ijamsville"
CONNECTICUT REVIEW "At the Altar"
HANGING LOOSE "Driving in the Midwest"
KENYON REVIEW "Unfinished Grief"
MICHIGAN QUARTERLY REVIEW "The Key"
NEW ENGLAND REVIEW "Now That We're Here"
THE NORTH AMERICAN REVIEW "Lightning Storm"and "Talia"
NOTRE DAME REVIEW "In the Sickroom"
PASSAGES NORTH "The Dead"
PITTSBURGH QUARTERLY REVIEW "Separation"
PRAIRIE SCHOONER "Picnic on Blue Hill" and "The Secrets of Trees"
PUERTO DEL SOL "Papusza: Roma Doll"
RATTLE "Noah"
RIVER STYX "What to Pack, What to Carry"
THE ANN STANFORD POETRY CONTEST "People of the Word"
SOUTHERN HUMANITIES REVIEW "Saboteurs;" "Old Grindleville Road;" and "Takes on a Birch Tree"
SOUTHERN POETRY REVIEW "Midnight Around Sligo Creek" (forthcoming)
SWINK "Dig"
THIRD COAST "Recovery"
BALANCING CHINA **(chapbook) Sow's Ear Press** "Unfinished Grief" and "Separation"
HARD CHARACTERS **(chapbook) March Street Press** "Saboteurs"

Contents

The Key	7
Morning Drive to Ijamsville	8
What to Pack, What to Carry	9
Papusza: Roma Doll	10
Dig	11
People of the Word	12
Saboteurs	13
Midnight Around Sligo Creek	14
Recovery	15
Driving in the Midwest	16
Picnic on Blue Hill	17
Lightning Storm	18
Noah	19
Talia	21
Separation	22
Unfinished Grief	23
The Old Grindleville Road	25
Thirst	26
At the Altar	27
Cantata	28
The Secrets of Trees	29
In the Sickroom	30
Now That We're Here	31
The Dead	32
Takes on a Birch Tree	33

The Key

Turncoat,
you think you're so
keen, think you know
how to penetrate the other
side, as if your fickle affinity
for playing favors weren't simply
appetite or habit. You may lunge
between the borders of open
and shut, may flex your
meddle but you've been
misplaced too many
times to trust,
your quisling
head turned
dull from
twisting
in a two-
bit two
step
with
your
own
ground
down
teeth.

Morning Drive to Ijamsville

Against overturned cups of rain,
the sharp distinction of holsteins
crunching their morning meal,
oblivious to Canadian geese
flying overhead. How glorious
to be a beast in unfurled weather,
to prod the men who hammer
the broken wooden fence
to finish their work faster.
While I navigate the weather,
nature plods on with its parade,
a gust of sunlight guzzling
through the flinching clouds.
The cows' colors hurt my eyes --
their white and black claims lie.
The rain, alone, tells the truth,
the bearing down neutral cry
of its gray, clear song
singing just how hard it is to see
through the falling sky, the threats
and hopes no color at all but
insistent see-through clarity, down,
down, so dark despite the early hour,
the rain reaches for what it cannot see
or stop, cupping its plentiful hands
to catch its own cold overspill.

What to Pack, What to Carry

An island is the earth's tongue. Tears of trees
ripple over the island. I am a suitcase
of eyes. On a train, studying the Island of Skye,
jagged line, bleat of letters, the island of ken,
islands of unborn bosoms of milk,
the island of smirched jabber, islands
of breath refusing to bring air.

A fetus spreads in my womb.
The pulp is soft, gutted and ripe.
Where does skin begin?
Stare deeply into water from the window.
See steeples of clouds loll their shoulders
on the pealing waves. Skin stops
in a clip-clop at the eyes,
those envelopes of indolent blue.

Where he handles me, I carry
the tears of arms growing
windwise on the heels of the sea.
It's the size of a small orange, he says.
Each leg, a shaking tree, weeps,
each hand drops a fruit,
my body a sack of fetid seeds.

Papusza: Roma Doll

We knew she wasn't ours
with her dark skin and blacker eyes
begging to be believed. Mama and
Papa wouldn't hear of our protests.
This is your new sister,
they commanded, scattering us
to our corners. The hut turned
into a factory of diapers and formula,
voices whispering late into evening,
even our shadows seemed to echo.
There was nothing to do but pet her
tiny legs and beg if this time
we could tip the bottle to her sucking lips.
Outside, the great war rolled over Hungary.
We learned to eat noodles and paprika
without chicken. Papa stopped
playing his violin. The baby grew bigger
and happier. I always wondered why
she would cock an ear toward falling
footsteps, whether she herself knew
she'd come to us from the forest,
her ears shining like foreign coins.

Dig

The prospector hollered *Go!* and we raised our shovels
as if we were one set of hands, the forward oomph
of our greed as good a fuel as any. It didn't matter
that no one had found any ore in these parts for ages,
we set about our work as if these repeating arms and legs
could reverse history. The sun dripped its reedy juice
over our heads, coating us with another shade of saffron.
Though the sound of shovels clawing into unforgiving soil
didn't offer any reassurance, we had long stopped listening
for ordinary human sounds, understood to mean, *Yes. Here.*
Stop. Our shadows grew longer than our bodies, as if
the upward arc of the shovels were lifting us skyward.
If there were any people that could remind us of ourselves,
we would not have recognized them, all the planets inching
closer to this dug-out valley. And still we kept digging.
Soon the birds were replaced by bats, the trees collapsed
inside their skins to bear up for another sleepless night.

People of the Word

It is the oldest story and someone has to tell it,
why shouldn't two brothers take turns taking
each other's blood, someone's got to shoot
the sun to claim the moon, when men want
what only women drop, eggs and the slippery
cycle of shore and border, blue because clouds
split at the teeth of line and green because fire
will always belong to rocks and right now the
storyline looks slanted but that's subjective
because between the hissing h in salaam and
shalom there's no shade, no syrup of dissonance.
Now the left hand saws off the right, eye for
an adam's apple and an eye toward the gate,
sizing up whatever is left in the garden, not
innocent olive trees but seeds, skins, not wadis
where an absence of water cries for what was
once a page. The author is out of control but
the story is the same, even condors don't look
here for scraps since earth and sky will bludgeon
it out until stones bleed and they will, when what
is lost means lavishing venom as if it were a wind
and not the ash it is. It is the oldest story and
someone has to read it to tell it and to tell it
someone has to know the difference between left
and right, fist and cup, beginning and ending, tear
and rip, when and why to turn the page. Someone
has to get lost in the desert but the two brothers
don't remember they are related, lost together
and all the rest of us implicated readers, our relative
luck to be on this side of the book but also a mirage,
like water in blood like gold in ore, because if rocks
are rubbed long enough before they are hurled,
they will take the whip of fire with them.

Saboteurs

We are driving toward the place
in the road where the mine
will blow up. Doesn't matter
that we planted it,
we're driving straight on
as if death were the next
errand on a Saturday list.
As if back then
we knew what
we were laying.

Now panic crashes in.
I can see you are screaming
but all I hear is silence
ticking, taking hold
in the back of my skull,
casting back to the start
before we'd made our plans,
before we knew that sabotage
demanded subjects. Back then,
a match kindled a candle wick.

Shifting into fifth gear,
you wrench the steering wheel.
The silence quickly springs
closer, louder. And just
then I'm nostalgic -
what if I've left the stove on?
There isn't time to turn around.
No, that's wrong,
there are buckets of time.
Exploding takes forever.

Midnight Around Sligo Creek

Tonight I take curves, pushing
the pedal through floors of darkness --
freefall of bushes and wind,
trill scattered to whoosh.

Flock of cars, fleet of bats
follow the same flight
that disappears and reappears.
Not an easy tugging at what isn't there,

I burn and shout, searching for room
through nettle and snakes, through
the socked-in dark, dry as chalk,
but wanting it wet, wet.

Recovery

Behind a drifting island
my last sun disappeared.
Now, to cast a wish,
tip toward rising smoke.

To track the wish,
watch the horizon
fold in to the sea,

vow to reverse intention --
use foam to remember,
follow ripples to forget,

become a wave
or a throat
opening and
closing,

ask questions
with small words.

Driving in the Midwest

must be heaven.
Steel silos cast
tall shadows
over the roads
between Wisconsin
and Minnesota.
As moon repeats sun,
endless fields might
as well be water.
Green draws
ripples of grass
against horizon's
purple rim and
Valley-Hi Drive-In
plays to an audience
of no one
but all the stars,
the sky, a steeple
here and there.

Picnic on Blue Hill

You drive me to touch the hill,
make me see that blue
is how the sky holds green.

Finches carol on the tips
of tall pine, lilacs
inspire the air.

With you I mine my name.
I open and the wind splashes
sacrum, sternum, weightless

neck, lifted off
the ground, dew
flickering in the grass.

Everywhere light
so startlingly frank
our eyes clench shut.

What kisses feed
fills me
on your tongue.

Lightning Storm

After exquisite love
I look for a breeze
to lay my boneless body on
below the field of humidity
that flags our wilted bed.
I try to leave the air, at least

lift the sweating sheet above
my body's heat, rippling, singed.
Plugged-in-the socket, electrical
charge, privy to delicious
collapse, impossibly light,
altogether exchanged.

I am still hot. My thighs beat.
Then suddenly, a second rain --
scallop-shaped, persistent --
plays the tin roof, and
lightning's claws snap,
clenching the synapses shut.

Tonight, our bodies wanted
the shortest path, as lightning
will strike what's highest in the field.
Luminous crisscrossed pile:
ankles, calves, kneecaps

delicately positioned
to discharge the charge,
remand the made, make
our terrifying closeness
to catching fire simply
a matter of weather or impulse.

Noah

The full moon falls away
as my five-day-old drifts
along the sifting waters of sleep.
He makes murmurous sounds
that rock his basket, a kayak
floating and falling through rain
that's flowed every night and day
since he was born.

In his generations, Noah alone was good.
He saved his family and the animals
from all the fountains of the deep.
In the seventh month his ark rested
upon the mountains of Ararat.
Rest Noah, quiet Noah, rest.

What compassion we grasp,
we give back in names.
The new moon falls through mist
as my month-old son forges
the currents of his patience.
He sleeps on and off and on
through thirty days and nights of rain,
pushing through water with his heavy head.

Each tiny, straining edge: jaw, cheek, chin --
above a body light as a candle.
Dreaming, his long fingers
ripple through caves and
weeping willows under water,
off angles of the air.

Milk has made him strong enough
to steer. His paddles dip and stir.

All of the creatures keep still
as the ark undulates and drifts.
Noah is not afraid of rain.
He swims toward the mountains.

Talia

(In Hebrew, God's dew)

Five days old, she already feels the burden
of her body, born with all the eggs she will
ever shed, eggs that will fall like the moon,
and she wakes with a mouth full of tears,
shaking her fist, singing sharply,
a shard of beach glass against stone.

And just when she is most difficult to calm,
an agéd smile creeps across her mouth.
She will keep her secrets. She listens
for every sound, as if each could explain
the mystery of birth, that record of tears,
the tears that stars weep

and turn into beads, those morning gems.
Inside every tear a hundred eggs sloughed,
inside every egg a hundred wishes growing.
And every month may teach her mercy.
Talia, wise, already
a woman waiting inside.

Separation

Last night I saw birds with human eyes,
the color of ash, birds taller than I,
were stalking me through old snow.
Their three-starred tracks didn't stay
and last night birds flew in my body.
I dreamt the inside of stars was milk
from every mother's breast, melting,
falling, till all the stars had vanished.
Birds flew south to start back up,
along the way they rescued stars.
Once I watched my mother and grandmother
as they stood beneath a window and wept.
Their chins lifted to the sky
nipples to an open beak.

Unfinished Grief

for Yoko Ono

A woman holds her weeping
braids, for hair is also
water falling. One woman
mourning is an unripe thicket.

*

A woman hisses at shadows
hiding in the fog.
Many women are an army,
tumbling through the fields.

*

A woman with small eyes
looks at her son, remembering bread.
But women are a circle of yeast.
Eggs shoot up in moist corners.

*

A woman runs after a knife,
trying to cut evenly. Women
prepare to bleed, folding
their batting, begetting.

*

A woman follows her voice,
screaming through alleys
as she collides into grief.
When women fall, they shatter.

*

A woman slit by glass
streams blood beneath
the moon's sticky glow.
Women forge a current from their pain.

*

A woman twists in water,
nipple to knee, thinking of nothing.
Women are the islands in a lake,
spongy earth pockets, pungent and warm.

*

A woman remembers to turn
on the oven as she begins
swimming out. Preservers
are holes. Our bodies are holes.

*

A woman
with small eyes
looks at her son,
remembering his father.

The Old Grindleville Road

Mushrooms the size of baseball caps,
ochre-colored umbrellas. And white
moss old as the corrupted deer skull
with cloud-colored teeth, packed under
leaves. Hemlocks and pine, blueberry
barrens and thump of twigs, everywhere
evergreen, and black bear, fishers,
loons and moose, an abandoned road
as wide as a man's outstretched arms,
that drifts up and down reluctant hills
past stone walls left from a village
that no longer exists, except for
its name, *Grindleville.* And when
you stop for a look, the no-see-ums
and ghosts swarm, a century past
in this parcel of land, forest so thick,
even the seller doesn't know the limits
of his own property. Cloud cover, pine
beds, books and books of trees, and
only the sound of the air
asking for a lift back to town.

Thirst

What does the horse in the field know
or the birds that swoop before my car
while I chase my heart, as if it were
a child that I could catch and scold?
Some things continue in spite of inattention:
my foot on the pedal,
my hands at ten and two.

Do animals know a thing as beginning or
ending? When I lie with my young children,
squeezing their anguish to mine,
their tight bodies know and keen,
rewinding to when I sobbed as a child,
to all the times you told me,
Who ever said life was fair?

What do the horse or birds know
about the difference between field and sky?
For each, their hunger only says: *Now*,
as when I feel the weight of your dying,
my foot presses the pedal harder
and I must weep *now*, *here*,
for the need to weep is also a hunger.

At the Altar

Watch how the wind
animates the still life
in a flurry of petals,
cherry blossom and dogwood
drifting like sunlight
across a rising creek,
pastels suspended
over macadam as if
gravity were a dare.
As if the altar were lowered,
and worship meant sailing
with wind on each quarter,
if watching the wind
through a window would
make one leave offerings
at the feet of weeping trees.

Cantata

When you are driving in a fleet of cars and
a train is coming in from the right
and an airplane is flying off to the left,
someone else is receiving bad news.
Every minute someone is picking up a telephone
as church bells toll for the giddy bride and groom,
as an ambulance rushes to the hospital just as
a woman grabs her child from the busy street.
While someone is being told the marriage is dead,
a boy and girl, for the first time, are finding the floor.
Every minute someone is not finding enough
water to drink, enough hope to eat. So much
depends on *is* and *will* every minute,
every minute someone is opening
the doctor's door to hear what radical cells have created,
as a grandfather helps his grandchild take her first step,
as the principal calls to say there's been an accident,
as a girl begins to bleed from her womb,
as a child finds the loaded gun his father left in the drawer.
And all of these minutes and their conjunctions
sure as the hand's first cry against a newborn's back.

The Secrets of Trees

The wig waits with the patience of a mushroom
while your scalp fights with your hair.
Only the tall oaks, braided and pocked, persist.
Reckless spendthrift, I count money on trees
and give myself to the barber's gossiping scissors;
you take poison to win your skirmish,
counting at each day's end a windfall of gratitude.
Still, the tall oaks that arch amidst the hickories--
in one place two trees growing from the same roots,
two different trunks, nuance of bark and holes--
know how to brush without hurting the air.
How lonely the human head without hair to hold it,
how bereft the daughter without her mother to plait
her hair. Where is she? Here, weeping at the feet
of oaks, here, fistfuls of longing, her bouquet of hair.

In the Sickroom

after a painting by Edvard Munch

When people wait, frozen to their grief
or their fear of the grief that will follow the news,
they lose their features, their fingers.
You can replace the door with a doctor
tipping his hat as he leaves the room,
or the shape of a chair with the sloping
shoulders of a heart-broken girl. You cannot
tell the difference between a shadow and its twin.

As if it were ordinary the doctor is always
leaving, melting into the doorway's mouth,
or that a portrait of Jesus hangs on the green wall
(as if green could resuscitate the waiting ones
and the dying one), next to the out-of-date calendar.
As if it were extraordinary these people
don't keen but keep their anguish close.
As if this tableau could breathe,

a woman grows out of a man's back, perhaps
a sister and brother, perhaps husband and wife.
She alone faces front, her hands two feckless shells
that barely touch her daughter's weeping braid.
Another woman, eager to help, curves over
their aged mother, whose white shawl covers her profile,
offering the only moment of light in the room.
The old man at the back twists his hands
to his bowed head, a flush coloring his pate.

These sculptures, these stones, each placed to absorb
the crashing grief, as if it were a runaway pigment.
Always there are seven people waiting for death:
the mother, the father, the son and his wife,
the daughter and her daughter, and the uninvited,
who will soon announce the close of visiting hours.
Seven sculptures of stone and all of their shadows
waiting in the sickroom to hear and unfreeze.

Now That We're Here

in the honesty room,
not a sentence is heard.
The doors have come down
with laryngitis. All the windows
keep their hands folded, even
the wallpaper is a wallflower
wilting under silence's grip.
Ordinarily a gossiping clutch,
the chairs sit without desire
to snicker or gesture.
The ignoble table, oblivious
to discord, holds court as if
this were any other day. Outside,
the wind burns and bangs
against the trees insinuating
themselves against the porch --
a neglected gutter hangs against
a branch, gathering a refuse
of leaves and lies. Now
the power will go out
and only a few candles
will raise their flames
to ask why, to ask when.

The Dead

don’t hear us when we picnic by the lake,
opening the squeaky basket of our summer lusts:
pineapple and prosciuto, tea biscuits
and brie, champagne that’s been on ice
until an hour ago, strawberries dressed in chocolate,
a sheet made from 100% Egyptian cotton
spread across the bank as if it were
a wave of billowing silk, and our favorite
books to occasionally open and quote from,
in between watching the children somersault
over the velvet field, enveloping their young brown arms
and legs, so that for a second we lose them in the rush
of green, but never scurry to our worst fears
that we’ve lost them for good, because the dead
are as far from here as the rings that circle Saturn,
the dead don’t smell the lilac bushes that infuse the air
or the perennials that add a hint of spice,
the dead don’t feel the cool water that kisses
our toes, our ankles, our knees until we sink
into the blueness of such relief we feel no weight,
no bottom or top, no difference between the waters
of the womb and the waters of our deaths.
The dead don’t hear the loons’ game of catch
with their echoing calls, don’t hear the wind
scratch the trees’ bitten branches, don’t
hear us call the children back from the lake
to leave before the light leaves us, but waltz
instead on feet that never tire, they dance
to piccolo and oboe, too dizzy and deaf
to care for us, as if spinning from Saturn
to Earth and back, they whirl like children
in a song about rings and never,
never turn light-headed.

Takes on a Birch Tree

Pink-splotched sky
ambles in through the marsh,
then trickles out toward red, orange,
yellow-topped trees to settle last on a birch
beginning to loosen. The tree begs to be forgiven
for surrendering to beavers, for riddling the shore with skin,
for dropping all the coins the sun shakes over the sand.
The birch no longer watches cliffs slough off clay
or how the cold teeth of the lake chew its trunk.
The water whips and snaps the indelicate
beach until all that remains are roots
sliding into the next crash
that always comes
from the same
wave.